Every Four Years (Almost)

The modern Olympic Summer Games have been held every four years since 1896, except during the two world wars. Connect the dots below to find what is carried from Athens, Greece, to each Olympic site. The dots can be connected in order by counting every four years. You will find the missing years.

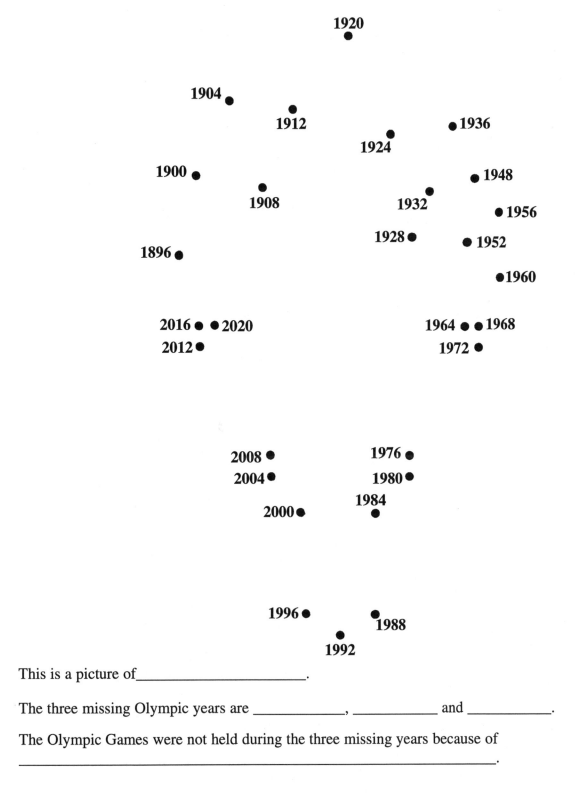

This is a picture of_____.

The three missing Olympic years are _____, _____ and _____.

The Olympic Games were not held during the three missing years because of

_____.

The Sports of the Olympic Summer Games

There are below 27 of the 29 sports in the modern Olympic Summer Games. Find them forwards, backwards, and diagonally, in the word search below.

```
S  C  C  M  D  D  G  D  B  C  V  L  T  V  L  D  Y  C  K  V  V  V  N  Y
C  D  Z  F  L  I  G  G  K  T  A  Q  O  W  S  P  V  A  N  J  M  O  W  D
W  J  B  W  B  D  V  N  S  P  H  N  L  H  W  C  R  R  C  C  L  L  X  H
T  R  A  C  K  &  F  I  E  L  D  H  O  C  K  E  Y  R  E  H  C  R  A  P
W  D  R  Q  C  G  N  C  N  T  X  O  P  E  X  L  V  C  T  C  T  Q  X  M
S  H  O  H  N  N  W  N  V  G  T  L  R  X  I  Y  L  A  L  S  C  I  J  S
L  C  W  C  E  I  B  E  B  I  L  B  E  J  Z  N  T  L  L  I  D  O  N  X
P  D  I  T  J  X  N  F  N  A  G  G  T  K  U  N  G  L  A  N  N  F  S  G
H  V  N  T  P  O  Y  G  B  O  N  B  A  M  E  D  L  A  B  N  A  G  W  Q
P  M  G  H  S  B  K  D  S  I  T  P  W  P  S  A  O  B  T  E  I  L  R  V
L  G  V  C  H  A  N  H  M  D  D  N  N  N  B  C  R  E  E  T  R  N  E  R
C  S  X  Y  D  A  N  M  T  C  G  R  I  Y  N  X  B  S  K  E  T  P  S  N
C  G  X  H  H  R  I  M  V  J  E  D  E  M  M  Z  D  A  S  L  S  Q  T  S
Z  K  T  M  J  W  Q  Y  Y  D  K  L  T  H  D  P  Y  B  A  B  E  F  L  D
T  L  A  Q  S  W  F  G  O  G  L  X  L  J  Y  A  S  Q  B  A  U  Y  I  B
R  E  J  V  J  M  V  M  S  O  B  L  W  K  G  J  B  D  L  T  Q  H  N  M
T  Q  K  B  W  Q  K  Y  V  G  N  I  T  F  I  L  T  H  G  I  E  W  G  Y
```

Cross off the words as you find them: archery, badminton, baseball, basketball, boxing, canoeing, cycling, diving, equestrian, fencing, field hockey, gymnastics, judo, modern pentathlon, rowing, shooting, soccer, swimming, table tennis, team handball, tennis, track & field, volleyball, water polo, weightlifting, wrestling, yachting

Eating Right for Health and Fitness

Directions: Cut out the foods pictured on the next page. Paste or tape them into the correct section on the food pyramid. Then you will see how many servings per day you should eat.

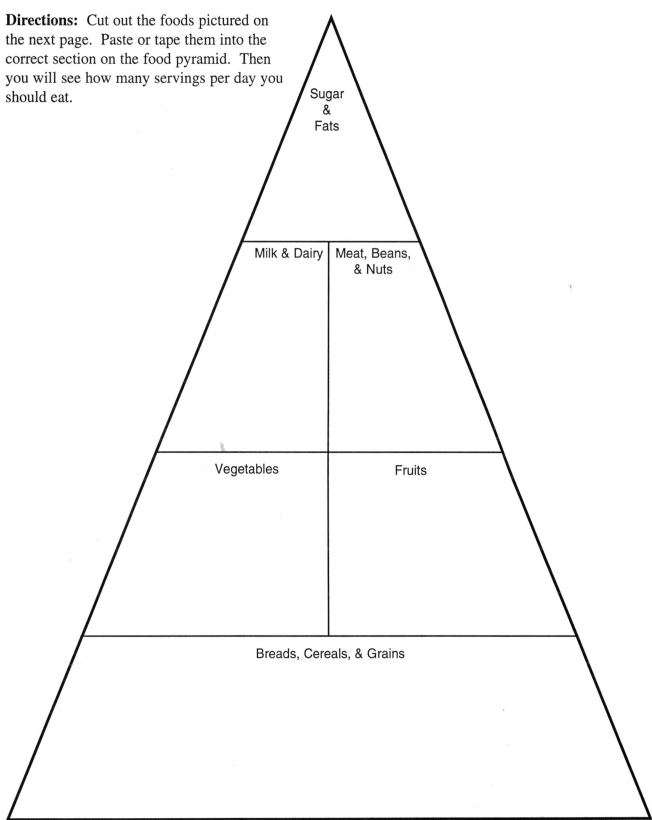

Sugar
&
Fats

Milk & Dairy | Meat, Beans, & Nuts

Vegetables | Fruits

Breads, Cereals, & Grains

Eating Right for Health and Fitness (cont.)

BREAD

VEGETABLE

MILK

FAT

FRUIT

GRAIN

VEGETABLE

BREAD

BREAD

FRUIT

CEREAL

DAIRY

BEANS

BREAD

FRUIT

MEAT

Crossword Puzzle

If you know your summer events, you will be able to solve this crossword in record Olympic time!

Across

1. In _____ athletes use a racket to compete.
6. _____ is a team sport similar to basketball and soccer, which is played in a pool.
8. In the sport of _____ a birdie is hit back and forth across a net.
10. The _____ participated in the sport of basketball.
12. In the sport of _____ one competes on the uneven parallel bars.
13. _____ is a sport for people who are not afraid of heights.

Down

2. The individual medley is a race in _____.
3. The decathlon combines ten _____ events.
4. A _____ is used when competing in fencing.
5. A coxswain steers a boat in the sport of _____.
7. _____ will be a spectator sport in Atlanta in 1996.
9. An _____ is achieved when the ball is served past the opposing team and remains in bounds.
11. Four runners together make up a _____.
12. Mark Spitz won seven _____ medals in the 1972 Olympic Summer Games.

Find Your Way to the Olympic Summer Games

Getting to the Olympic Games is not easy. Enter the maze at the Start Gate, then trace the path that will take you to the Olympic Summer Games.

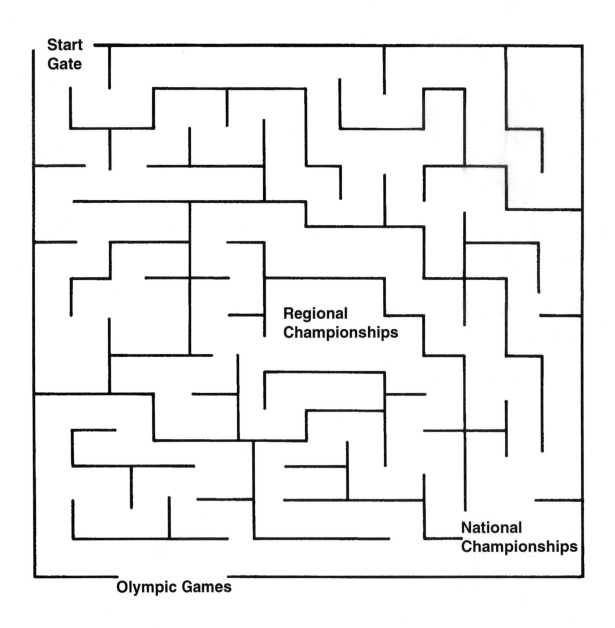

The U.S. Olympic Committee Flag

Use the code below to color the sections in the picture.

What do you see?_____

☆ white   ▲ red

✗ blue   ○ yellow

☐ black   ● green

Scrambled Games

Unscramble the name of each Olympic Summer event. Then find a place for it on the crossword puzzle below. Use the key letters to help.

1. raeryhc _____

2. akbatlbesl _____

3. gbnoix _____

4. gcnaineo _____

5. gsycmintas _____

6. sghnoiot _____

7. stienn _____

8. yganciht _____

Let the Games Begin

The Olympic flame can be traced back to the games of the ancient Greeks. The climax of Opening Ceremonies was a foot race where the winning runner would light the sacrificial fire opening the Games. This tradition was reinstituted in the Berlin Games of 1936, where a runner holding a torch, lit the Olympic flame. Today, the Olympic torch makes an elaborate journey from Athens, Greece, to the Olympic site in order to officially open the Games. **Directions:** Using the world map, plot a course for the Olympic torch starting in Athens, Greece, and ending in Atlanta, Georgia, for the 1996 Olympic Games. Make a list of the countries, states, and cities the torch will pass through.

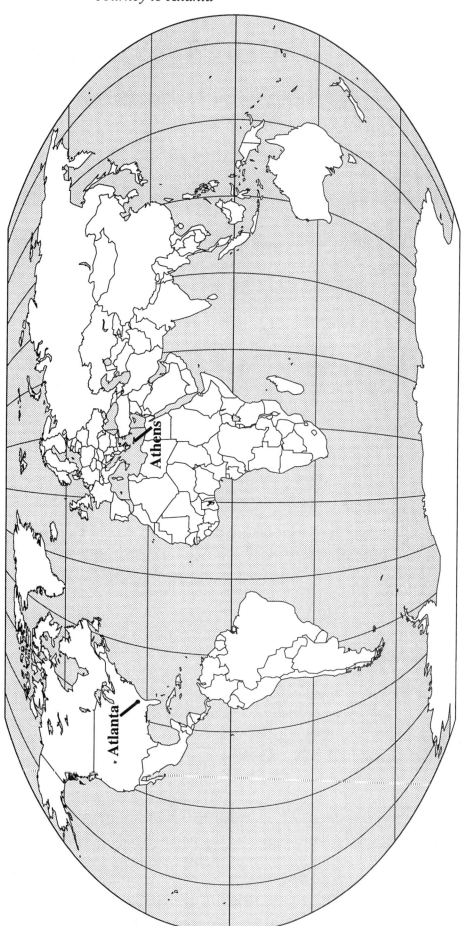

Sports & Events

This activity is based on the Olympic Games and Olympic Winter Games.

Directions: Mark the letter of the sport next to each corresponding statement. Some sports may be used more than once.

_____ 1. In what sport did Mark Spitz win seven gold medals and set seven world records?

_____ 2. Nadia Comaneci was the first person to score a perfect 10 in this sport at the Olympic Games.

_____ 3. Sonja Henie won the first of her three gold medals in what sport at the 1928 Olympic Winter Games in St. Moritz?

_____ 4. Abebe Bikila won his first of two gold medals while running barefoot through the streets of Rome competing in this event.

_____ 5. In 1988, at the Seoul Games, Kristen Otto won six gold medals, the most ever won by a woman in any sport in a single Olympic Games.

_____ 6. In 1984, at the Los Angeles Games, Joan Benoit Samuelson won a gold medal in this first ever women's event.

_____ 7. During the Olympic Winter Games of 1984, Bill Johnson became the only American male to ever win a gold medal in this event.

_____ 8. In 1988, Gao Min of China became the first female Olympic athlete ever to score more than 600 points in the springboard competition. What sport is it?

_____ 9. After several Olympic competitions, Dan Jansen finally won gold in this sport at Lillehammer.

_____10. What U.S. team accomplished one of the greatest upsets in sports history during the Olympic Winter Games of 1980 by winning the gold medal?

_____11. Jean-Claude Killy dominated this sport during the late 60s. He is also one of only two men to sweep all three of these events at a single Olympic Games.

_____12. The tropical island nation of Jamaica sent a team to compete in this sport in the Olympic Winter Games of 1988.

_____13. In what sport did Florence Griffith Joyner (Flo-Jo) win three gold medals along with setting one world record?

_____14. One of the most famous couples in modern Olympic history is Jayne Torvill and Christopher Dean of Great Britain. What sport did they compete in?

_____15. Picabo Street has become a well-known athlete because of her silver-medal performance in this sport at the Olympic Winter Games in Lillehammer.

a. gymnastics

b. skiing

c. track & field

d. marathon

e. swimming

f. bobsledding

g. ice dancing

h. speed skating

i. ice hockey

j. diving

k. figure skating

The Olympic Wheel

Every four years the events of the Olympic Summer Games provide the world's greatest athletes the opportunity to set and break Olympic and world records, to achieve the pinnacles in their sports, and to be written into history books. The Olympic wheel you will be creating provides historic events and highlights from every sport of the Olympic Games.

Materials Needed to Make an Olympic Wheel

- crayons or colored markers
- several paper fasteners
- scissors
- Olympic wheel patterns, pages 12–15 (You may want to reproduce pattern pages on heavy stock paper.)

Directions:

1. Cut out the circle patterns on pages 12 and 13. These will be the top and bottom of your Olympic wheel.
2. On each wheel, cut out the box where it says "Olympic Highlights."
3. Using your crayons or markers, color the medal patterns on pages 12 – 15.
4. After you are finished coloring, cut out the medal patterns and place them back-to-back.
5. Then, taking both wheels, put them on top of the medal patterns, making sure the statements fit within the Olympic highlights box.
6. Finally, using a paper fastener attach all four circles together through the middle. Your Olympic wheel is complete.

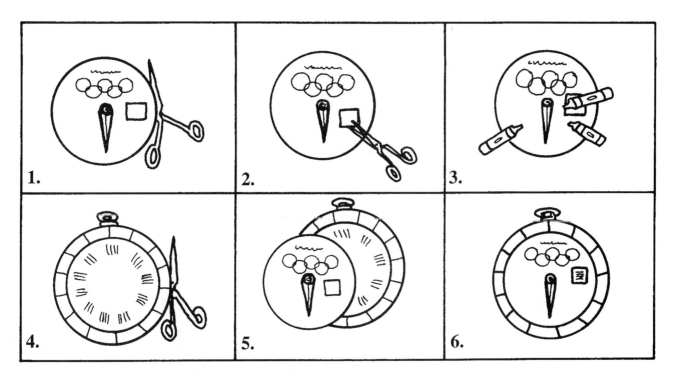

The Olympic Wheel (cont.)

The Olympic Wheel (cont.)

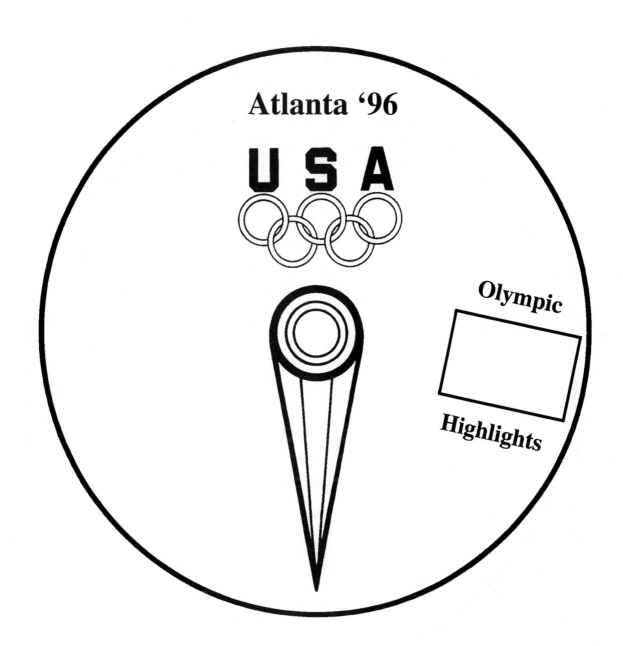

Atlanta '96

U S A

Olympic

Highlights

The Olympic Wheel (cont.)

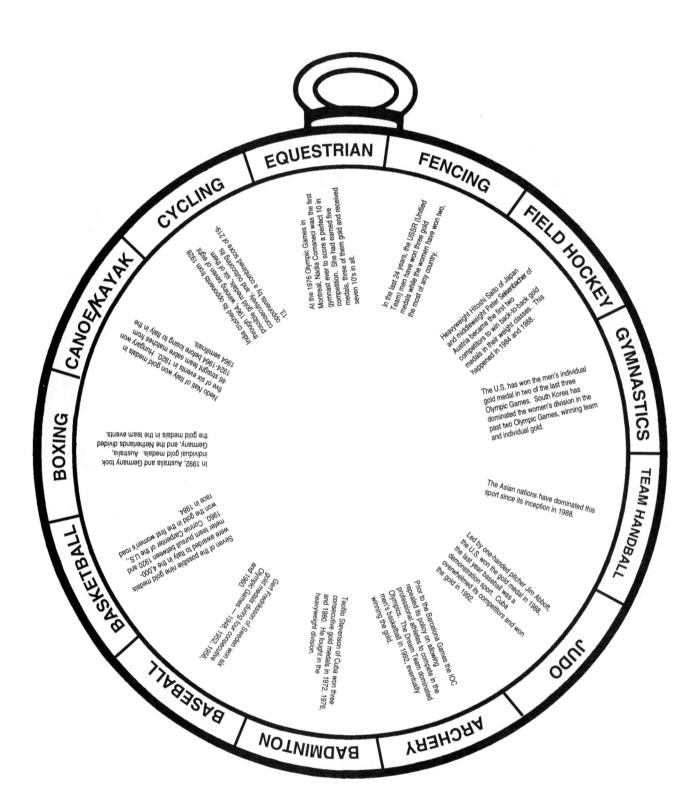

EQUESTRIAN

At the 1976 Olympic Games in Montreal, Nadia Comaneci was the first gymnast ever to score a perfect 10 in competition. She had earned five medals, three of them gold and received seven 10's in all.

FENCING

In the last 24 years, the USSR (Unified Team) men have won three gold medals while the women have won two, the most of any country.

FIELD HOCKEY

Heavyweight Hitoshi Saito of Japan and middleweight Peter Seisenbacher of Austria became the first two competitors to win back-to-back gold medals in their weight classes. This happened in 1984 and 1988.

GYMNASTICS

The U.S. has won the men's individual gold medal in two of the last three Olympic Games. South Korea has dominated the women's division in the past two Olympic Games, winning team and individual gold.

TEAM HANDBALL

The Asian nations have dominated this sport since its inception in 1988.

JUDO

Led by one-handed pitcher Jim Abbott, the U.S. won the gold medal in 1988, the last year baseball was a demonstration sport. Cuba overwhelmed its competitors and won the gold in 1992.

ARCHERY

Prior to the Barcelona Games the IOC repealed its policy on allowing professional athletes to compete in the Olympics. The Dream Team dominated men's basketball in 1992, eventually winning the gold.

Teofilo Stevenson of Cuba won three consecutive gold medals in 1972, 1976, and 1980. He fought in the heavyweight division.

BADMINTON

Gert Fredriksson of Sweden won six consecutive gold medals during four consecutive Olympic Games — 1948, 1952, 1956, and 1960.

BASEBALL

Seven of the possible nine gold medals were awarded to Italy in the 4,000-meter team pursuit between 1920 and 1960. Connie Carpenter of the U.S. won the gold in the first women's road race in 1984.

BASKETBALL

In 1992, Australia and Germany took individual gold medals. Australia, Germany, and the Netherlands divided the gold medals in the team events.

BOXING

Nedo Nadi of Italy won gold medals in five of six events in 1920. Hungary won 46 straight team sabre matches from 1924-1964 before losing to Italy in the 1964 semifinals.

CANOE/KAYAK

India crushed its opponents by a possible 1964, winning seven of eight consecutive gold medals, ski; or them through 1964, winning seven of eight combined score of 219.

13.

CYCLING

The Olympic Wheel (cont.)

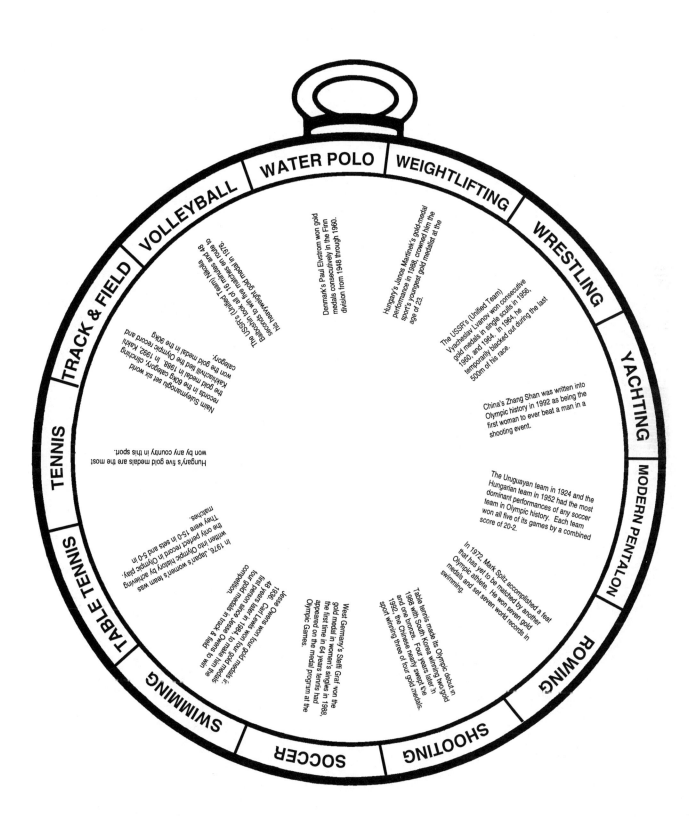

WATER POLO · WEIGHTLIFTING · WRESTLING · YACHTING · MODERN PENTALON · ROWING · SHOOTING · SOCCER · SWIMMING · TABLE TENNIS · TENNIS · TRACK & FIELD · VOLLEYBALL

Denmark's Paul Elvstrom won gold medals consecutively in the Finn division from 1948 through 1960.

Hungary's Janos Martinek's gold-medal performance in 1988, crowned him the sport's youngest gold medalist at the age of 23.

The USSR's (Unified Team) Vracheslav Lvanov won consecutive gold medals in single sculls in 1956, 1960, and 1964. In 1964, he temporarily blacked out during the last 500m of his race.

China's Zhang Shan was written into Olympic history in 1992 as being the first woman to ever beat a man in a shooting event.

The Uruguayan team in 1924 and the Hungarian team in 1952 had the most dominant performances of any soccer team in Olympic history. Each team won all five of its games by a combined score of 20-2.

In 1972, Mark Spitz accomplished a feat that has yet to be matched by another Olympic athlete. He won seven gold medals and set seven world records in swimming.

Table tennis made its Olympic debut in 1988 with South Korea winning two gold and one bronze. Four years later in 1992, the Chinese nearly swept the sport winning three of four gold medals.

West Germany's Steffi Graf won the gold medal in women's singles in 1988, the first time in 64 years tennis had appeared on the medal program at the Olympic Games.

1936: Carl Lewis won four gold medals 48 years later in 1984, to make him the first person since Jesse Owens to win four gold medals in track & field competition.

Jesse Owens won four gold medals in 1936.

In 1976, Japan's women's team was written into Olympic history by achieving the only perfect record in Olympic play. They were 15-0 in sets and 5-0 in matches.

Hungary's five gold medals are the most won by any country in this sport.

The USSR's (Unified Team) Nikolai Balbosiin took all of 16 minutes and 48 seconds to win five matches en route to his heavyweight gold medal in 1976.

Naim Suleymanoglu set six world records in the 60kg category, clinching the gold medal in 1988. In 1992, Kakhi Kakhiachvilli tied the Olympic record and won the gold medal in the 90kg category.

Answer Key

Page 1

This picture is a <u>torch</u>

The three missing Olympic years are <u>1916, 1940, and 1944</u>

The Olympic Games were not held during the three missing years because of <u>World War I (1916) and World War II (1940 and 1944)</u>

Page 2

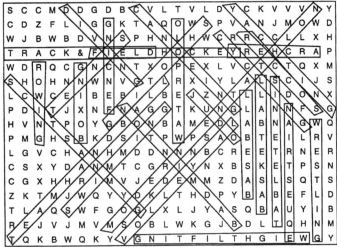

Which two sports were not in the puzzle? They were softball and syncronized swimming

Page 3

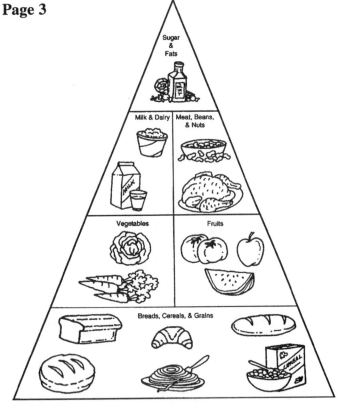

Page 5

(crossword puzzle)

TENNIS, WATERPOLO, ROWING, TRACK & FIELD, BADMINTON, DREAMTEAM, GYMNASTICS, DIVING

Page 7

You see the rings on the Olympic flag

Page 8

1. archery
2. basketball
3. boxing
4. canoeing
5. gymnastics
6. shooting
7. tennis
8. yachting

Page 10

1. swimming (e)
2. gymnastics (a)
3. figure skating (k)
4. marathon (d)
5. swimming (e)
6. marathon (d)
7. downhill skiing (b)
8. diving (j)
9. speed skating (h)
10. ice hockey (i)
11. skiing (b)
12. bobsledding (f)
13. track & field (c)
14. ice dancing (g)
15. skiing (b)